Awfy Braw!

OOR WULLIE FUNBOOKS

KT-375-078

OOR WULLIE

There's ice cream doon this laddie's back.
His foot is hurtin', too.
But guess who's makin' others laugh —
That's right it's You-Know-Who!

I'VE NOTHIN' TAE DAE!

MICHTY! A'BODY'S DAEIN' GUID DEEDS THE DAY, EXCEPT ME!

CAN I GIE YE A HELP, MRS WULSON?

A HELP? OH — WEEL, AYE — I SUPPOSE YE CAN, IF YE REALLY WANT TO.

YE CAN WASH THE DISHES.

CRIVVENS! THAT SOAPY WATER'S AFFY SLIPPERY!

SKITE

DIVE

CAUGHT YE OOF!

DUNT!

SAVE

HELP! MA DOSE IS STUCK IN THE KEYHOLE!

HANG ON, WULLIE I'M COMIN'!

THAT'S IT — YE'LL BE SAFER DOIN' A BIT O' POLISHING!

OOYAH!

OH DEAR!

BUMP

I TELL YE WHAT — YE CAN TRY TIDYING OUT THIS CUPBOARD.

What do you get
if you cross a football team
with an ice cream?

Aston Vanilla!

Now, ASK YOUR FRIEND TO THINK OF ANY NUMBER FROM 1 TO 9. TELL HIM TO MULTIPLY IT BY 3 AND THEN ADD 6.

NEXT, TELL HIM TO DIVIDE THE RESULT BY 3 AND FINALLY TO SUBTRACT THE NUMBER HE FIRST THOUGHT OF.

YOU CAN IMMEDIATELY TELL HIM THE RESULT BECAUSE THE ANSWER WILL ALWAYS BE 2. TRY IT!

OOR WULLIE
SECRET AGENT
0003½

Figure-FUN

7·11·12·13·14·16·19·20·21

WRITE THE NINE GIVEN NUMBERS, ONE IN EACH CIRCLE, SO THAT EACH OF THE THREE SIDES OF THE TRIANGLE WILL ADD TO 58.

Double Trouble!

IF YOU PRINT THE CORRECT WORDS IN THE BOXES ACROSS, THE SAME WORDS WILL READ DOWNWARDS.

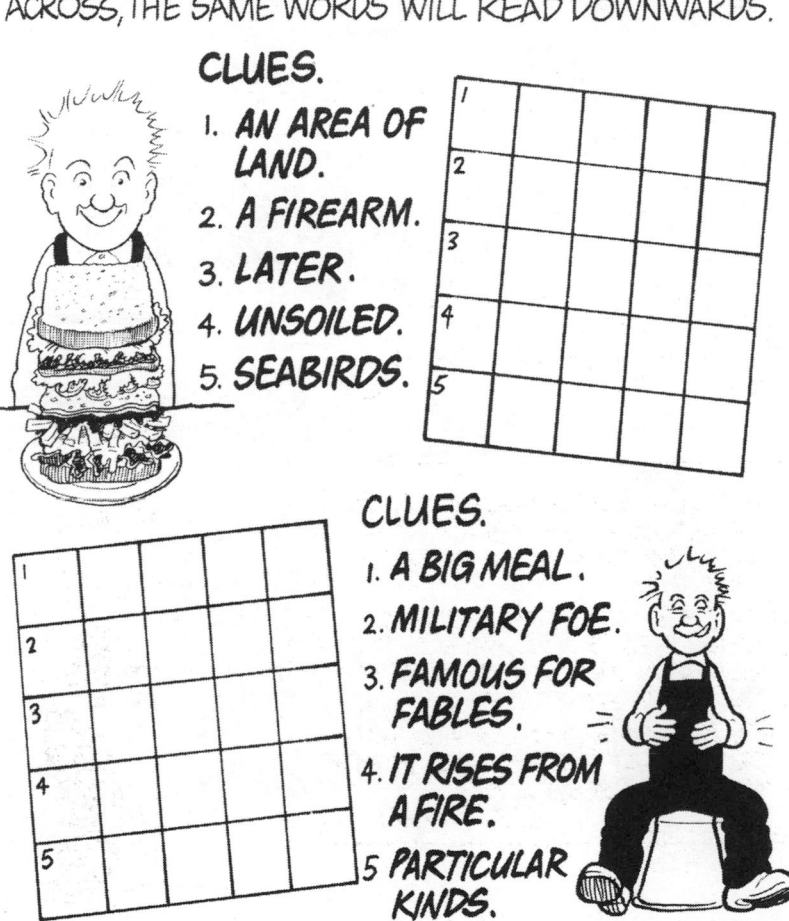

CLUES.

1. AN AREA OF LAND.
2. A FIREARM.
3. LATER.
4. UNSOILED.
5. SEABIRDS.

CLUES.

1. A BIG MEAL.
2. MILITARY FOE.
3. FAMOUS FOR FABLES.
4. IT RISES FROM A FIRE.
5. PARTICULAR KINDS.

ANSWERS
First square: 1. Tract. 2. Rifle. 3. After. 4. Clean. 5. Terns.
Second Square: 1. Feast. 2. Enemy. 3. Aesop. 4. Smoke. 5. Types.

ANSWERS:— 1.ARBROATH. 2.ROTHESAY. 3.ST.ANDREWS. 4.HELENSBURGH. 5.PORTOBELLO. 6.LARGS.

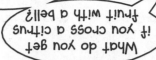

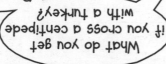

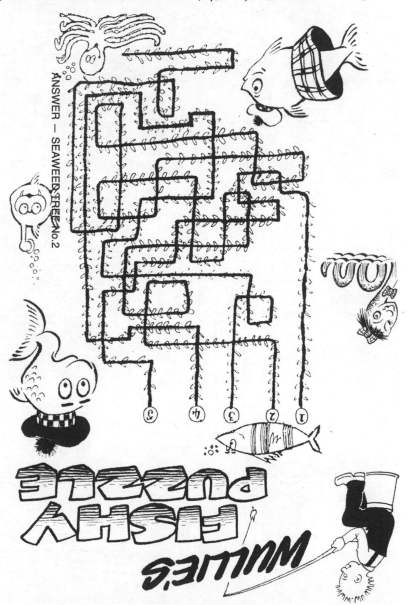

Can you help Freddy Fish choose the right seaweed tree to find his way to his friend Ollie the Octopus?

ANSWER — SEAWEED TREE No.2

WULLIE'S FISHY PUZZLE

Name That Toon

Reading across, print a letter in each blank square to spell the names of eight places in Scotland.

Certain letters have been written in to help you.

Answers — GLASGOW; LAURENCEKIRK; BRORA; PORTSOY; SELKIRK; MALLAIG; KINGUSSIE; ARDROSSAN.

FUNNY

What's Next?

THE FACES IN THE DRAWING ARE PUT TOGETHER IN A CERTAIN PATTI_____ES VERY CAREFULLY, AND SEE IF YOU CAN FIND THE MISSING FACE.

ANSWER — A WHITE CIRCLE

Answer – A white circle

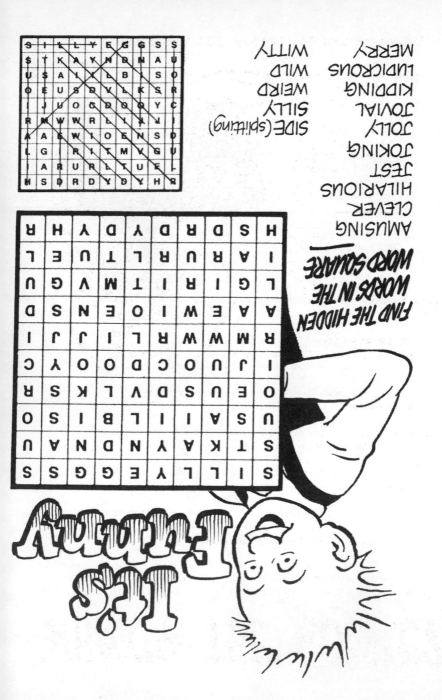

FIND THE HIDDEN
WORDS IN THE
WORD SQUARE

AMUSING
CLEVER
HILARIOUS
JEST
JOKING
JOLLY
JOVIAL
KIDDING
LUDICROUS
MERRY
SIDE (splitting)
SILLY
WEIRD
WILD
WITTY

It's
Funny

WHAT'S THE SCORE?

In this quiz, Wullie has given you a choice of answers. At the end of the quiz, add up your scores and see how well you have done. No cheatin'!

1. What is a canteloupe? (a) vegetable (b) drink (c) fruit

2. Picasso was a famous (a) singer (b) artist (c) actor

3. Which is the odd one out? (a) stetson (b) jodhpurs (c) sombrero

4. Which sport is played at Twickenham? (a) golf (b) tennis (c) rugby

5. How many players are there in an American football team? (a) 15 (b) 11 (c) 13

6. Who would use a stethoscope? (a) a sailor (b) a doctor (c) an explorer.

7. Lisbon is the capital of which country? (a) Portugal (b) Austria (c) Spain

8. What is a baby elephant called? (a) a pup (b) a calf (c) a cub

9. Who played Hagrid in Harry Potter and the Philospher's Stone? (a) Billy Connolly (b) Robert Carlyle (c) Robbie Coltrane

10. What is a samosa? (a) an Indian snack (b) a flower (c) a boat

Answers 1.(c) 2.(b) 3.(b) 4.(c) 5.(b) 6.(b) 7.(a) 8.(b) 9.(c) 10.(a).

ANSWER — No.3

AFTER STUDYING THE FACES IN THE PICTURES CAREFULLY, CAN YOU DECIDE WHICH OF THE FACES NUMBERED 1 to 6 SHOULD BE USED TO COMPLETE THE LOGICAL SEQUENCE.

FEATURE Pages

Drink Up

FIND THE MISSING WORDS

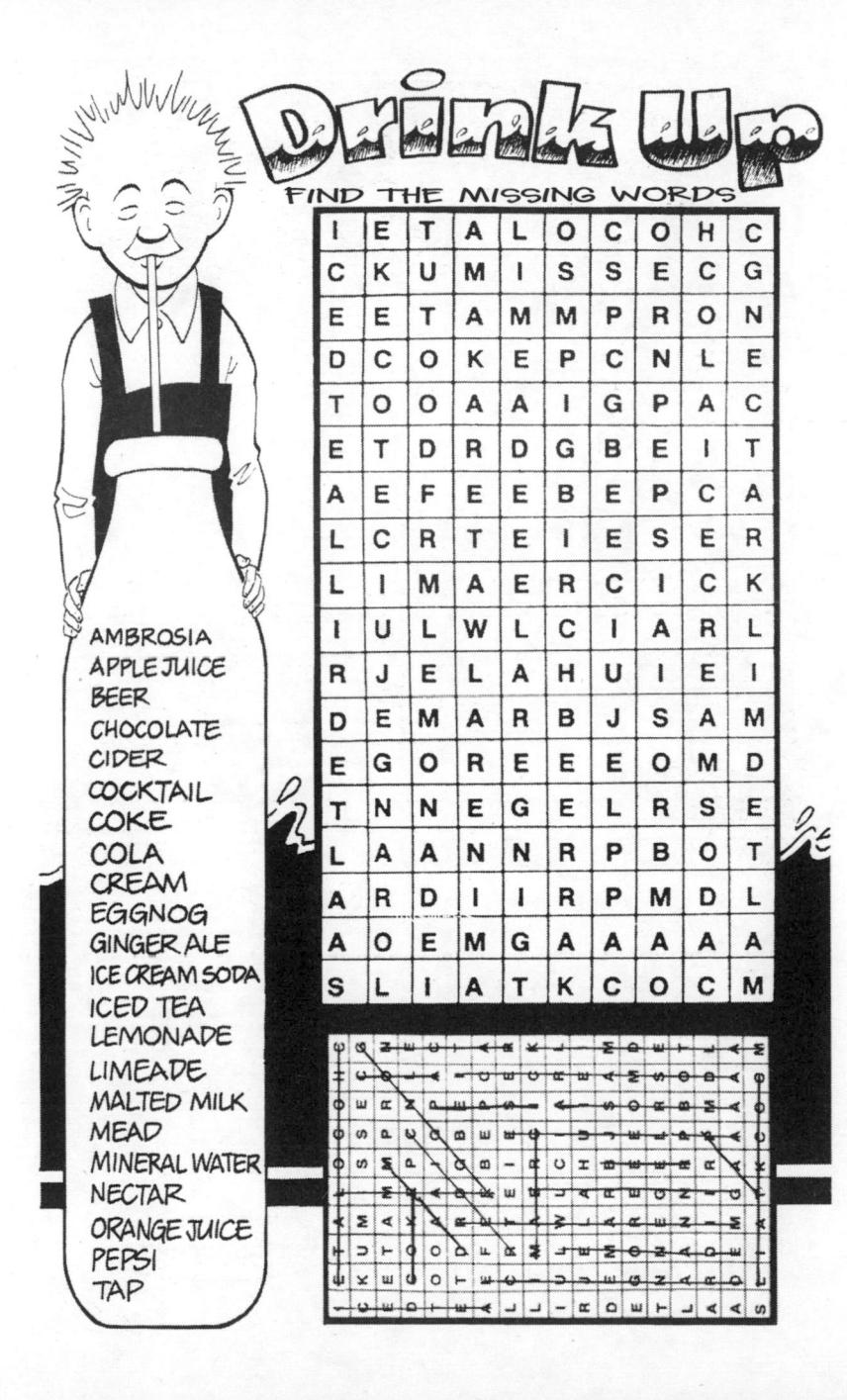

AMBROSIA
APPLE JUICE
BEER
CHOCOLATE
CIDER
COCKTAIL
COKE
COLA
CREAM
EGGNOG
GINGER ALE
ICE CREAM SODA
ICED TEA
LEMONADE
LIMEADE
MALTED MILK
MEAD
MINERAL WATER
NECTAR
ORANGE JUICE
PEPSI
TAP

I	E	T	A	L	O	C	O	H	C
C	K	U	M	I	S	S	E	C	G
E	E	T	A	M	M	P	R	O	N
D	C	O	K	E	P	C	N	L	E
T	O	O	A	A	I	G	P	A	C
E	T	D	R	D	G	B	E	I	T
A	E	F	E	E	B	E	P	C	A
L	C	R	T	E	I	E	S	E	R
L	I	M	A	E	R	C	I	C	K
I	U	L	W	L	C	I	A	R	L
R	J	E	L	A	H	U	I	E	I
D	E	M	A	R	B	J	S	A	M
E	G	O	R	E	E	E	O	M	D
T	N	N	E	G	E	L	R	S	E
L	A	A	N	N	R	P	B	O	T
A	R	D	I	I	R	P	M	D	L
A	O	E	M	G	A	A	A	A	A
S	L	I	A	T	K	C	O	C	M

THERE'S A CHAP AT THE DOOR!

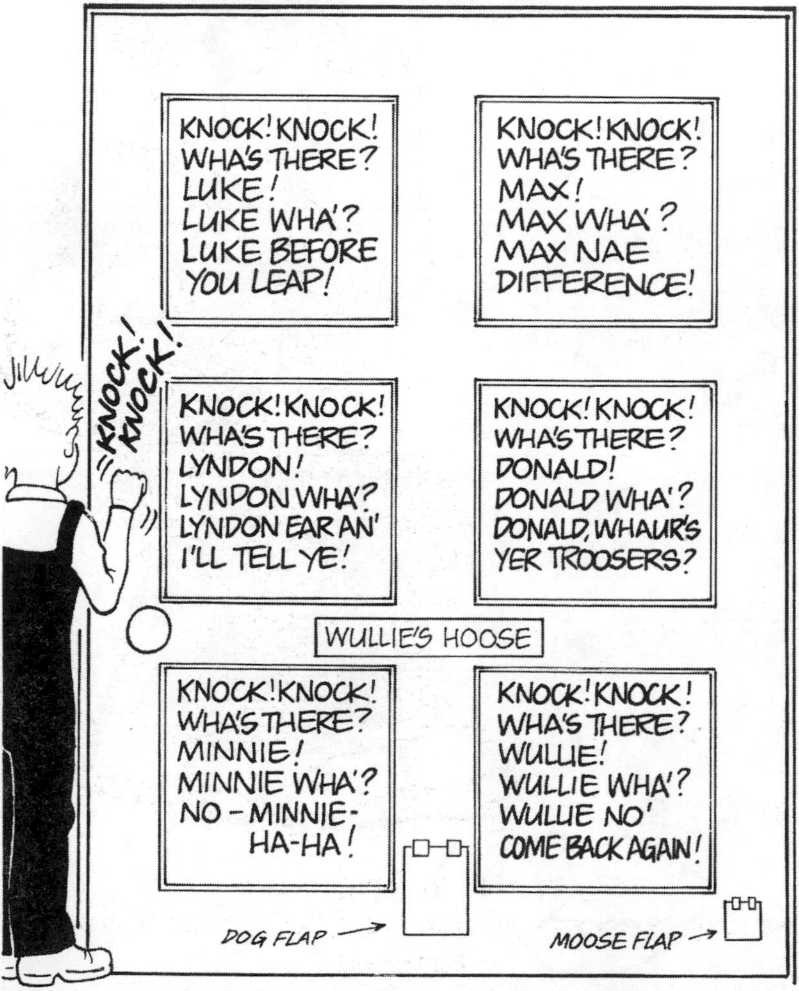

ISLAND HOPPING!

Willie's going on a tour of the Scottish islands. Fill in the missing letters to discover which islands he'll visit!

1. A _ _ A _
2. I _ L _ Y
3. M _ _ L
4. L E W I S
5. O R K N E Y
6. S H E T L A N D
7. J _ R _
8. B U _ _
9. E _ G _
10. R _ M

ANSWERS

1. Arran. 2. Islay 3. Mull. 4. Lewis. 5. Orkney 6. Shetland.
7. Jura. 8. Bute. 9. Eigg. 10 Rum

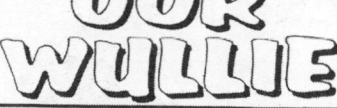

OOR WULLIE

Nae pals tae play wi' — that's a shame.
But trust oor lad — he's cunning!
He knows exactly what it takes
Tae bring his three chums running!

I THINK I'LL GO AN' SEE MY PALS.

BUT ——

SORRY, WULLIE. ECK'S OOT SOMEWHERE.

AND ——

BOB'S NO' IN, WULLIE. I DINNA KEN WHAUR HE IS.

THEN —— SORRY, WULLIE, SOAPY'S . . .

SAVE YER BREATH, MRS SOUTAR. I GET THE MESSAGE.

WHIT A SCUNNER. I'LL JUST HAE TAE PLAY BY MASEL'!

THAT'S IT, WULLIE —— ROOND THE CENTRE-HALF . . .

DRIBBLE

. . . NOW SHOOT!

GOAL!

ACH, IT'S NO' THE SAME WINNIN' AGAINST NAEBODY!

RACE YE TAE THE CORNER, SHADOW!

READY, STEADY ——

Why were the two elephants thrown off the beach?

Because between them they only had a single pair of trunks!

HARRY COME HOME

HAVE FUN WITH YOUR FRIENDS, SEEING HOW QUICKLY YOU CAN GET HARRY BACK HOME. USING THESE BONES AS COUNTERS, YOU NEED A SIX TO START.

A B C D

START 1 2 3 4 5

23 24 25 26 STOPPED TO CHASE CAT. MISS A TURN. 27 28 29

30 RAN AFTER BALL. FORWARD 3 SPACES. 31 32 33 34 35 36 BEG FOOD. MISS THREE TURNS.

37 38 39 40 41 42

ANSWERS — High-heeled shoe; Indian head-dress; Broken glass pane; Rugby ball; Mohican haircut; Cat on wall; Missing bricks on wall; Spots on ball; Hair on Mr Mildew; Long trousers on boy.

SPOT THE DIFFERENCE!

There are 10 differences between the pictures. Can you find them all?

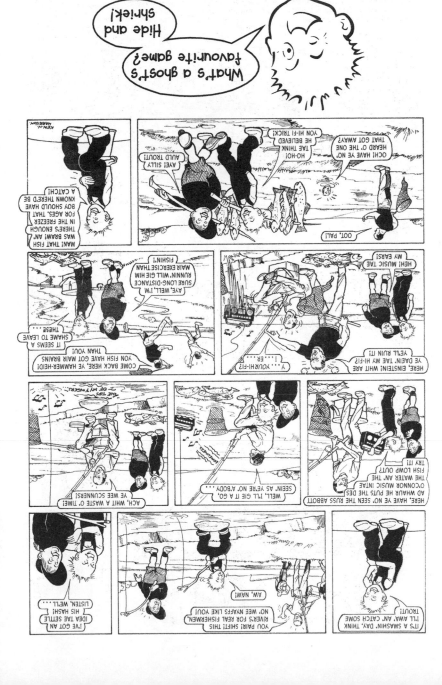

WALLIE'S SUMA GRAN

(WULLIE'S ANAGRAMS)

Here are a few anagrams to get you started. Unscramble the groups of letters shown on the left, to spell out the answers to the clues opposite. Numbers (in brackets) indicate the number of words. This should clear the cobwebs from the old brainbox!

1. PUSSY DONE THAT (3)
2. KIS THE CUB (2)
3. IM ROSE TRAPPERSON (2)
4. ORB HAD NO PEN (2)
5. PUM C CHORD (2)
6. WEARY HER (2)
7. CRY URCHIN ECK (2)
8. REBEL ST CHINA DUG (2)
9. I CLEP RAIL ACE (1)
10. LOCH PRITY (1)
11. DRAW TOON TEETH (3)
12. BART HINE (2)
13. STRAY MONROE (2)
14. SECOND TAG RAMBLES TOG (2)

CLUES

Wullie's favourite reading.
His place to relax.
Wull's favourite person?
A rose from number 10 Glebe Street.
The long arm of . . .
Faithful friend.
Friday night supper treat.
A Capital classic.
Wullie's favourite Scottish group.
Wull's Perthshire holiday destination.
Where he went last year, Clydeside.
Granpaw Broon's pin-up lass.
Two-Scottish soccer sides.
Breakfast. Your brain might feel a bit like this by now.

ANSWERS:
1 THE SUNDAY POST. 2 HIS BUCKET. 3 PRIMROSE PATERSON. 4 DAPHNE BROON. 5 PC MURDOCH. 6 WEE HARRY. 7 CHICKEN CURRY. 8 EDINBURGH CASTLE. 9 CAPERCAILLIE. 10 PITLOCHRY. 11 DOON THE WATTER. 12 THE BAIRN. 13 AYR, MONTROSE. 14 SCRAMBLED EGG ON TOAST.

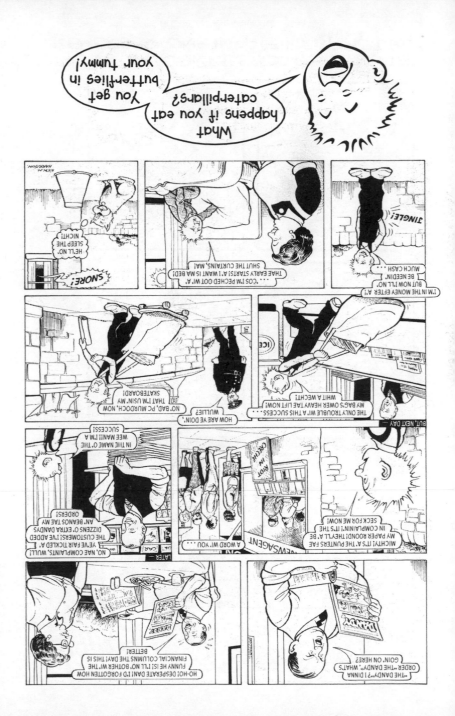

Answer - No.5

ANSWER — No.5

Wullie's ROPE TRICK

Gone fishing!

Wullie wants to go fishing on a Scottish loch, but he's not sure which one. Fill in the missing letters and help him make up his mind.

1. Loch –innhe

2. Loch – unart

3. Loch – ay

4. Loch – omond

5. Loch – yne

6. Loch –ong

7. Loch – annoch

8. Loch –even

9. Loch – ourn

10. Loch – ess

1. Loch Linnhe. 2. Loch Sunart. 3. Loch Tay. 4. Loch Lomond. 5. Loch Fyne. 6. Loch Long. 7. Loch Rannoch 8. Loch Leven. 9. Loch Hourn 10. Loch Ness.
Answers

FASCINATING FACTS

THE MOST PROLIFIC MOUSE-CATCHER OF ALL-TIME WAS 'TOWSER', THE RESIDENT TORTOISESHELL CAT AT GLEN TURRET DISTILLERY IN CRIEFF, SCOTLAND. BETWEEN 1963 AND HER SAD DEATH IN 1987, TOWSER CAUGHT THE GRAND TOTAL OF 28,899 MICE!

IN JUNE 1746 BONNIE PRINCE CHARLIE ESCAPED TO SKYE WITH FLORA MacDONALD. FOR SAFETY HE WENT IN THE DISGUISE OF AN IRISH MAID NAMED BETTY BURKE, AND WORE A FLOWERY FROCK AND APRON!

THE LONGEST RECORDED DISTANCE FOR THROWING A HAGGIS IS 163 FT 9½ INCHES, BY ALAN PETTIGREW, AT THE ARDROSSAN HIGHLAND GAMES ON JUNE 14th, 1981.

MANY YEARS AGO, AN EDINBURGH COURT HEARD THE TALE OF THE ROBOT WINE WAITER THAT RAN AMOK IN A RESTAURANT, KNOCKING OVER FURNITURE AND TERRIFYING DINERS, UNTIL ITS HEAD FELL OFF INTO A CUSTOMER'S LAP!

IT WAS IN 1692 THAT A GOVERNMENT FORCE TRIED TO WIPE OUT THE MacDONALDS IN THE GLENCOE MASSACRE. TO THIS DAY THE NINE OF DIAMONDS IS KNOWN AS THE 'CURSE OF SCOTLAND' BECAUSE THE CARD RESEMBLES THE ARMS OF THE MASTER OF STAIR, WHO WAS HELD RESPONSIBLE FOR THE SLAUGHTER.

FOOD ANAGRAMS

Unscramble the groups of letters shown to spell out some of Wullie's favourite grub. Numbers in brackets indicate the number of words. Go on — get yer teeth intae this!

	CLUES
1. MICE EAT D ANTS TIN (3)	Wullie's famous and favourite tea
2. FOILING BEEB (2)	Often in Grannie's soup
3. AN SHEEPI AND GGS (3)	Rabbie Burns
4. BOTH SCORTCH (2)	Ma's Sunday soup
5. PET O HUGH DOT (2)	Found in wee tubs — ask yer mum
6. DUMPLING PUD (2)	Xmas treat
7. EEL ICY JEEP (2)	Wull's favourite bread snack
8. JEEMY LEARN CC DIAL (4)	Nice on hot day
9. TAN NOSE BOAST (3)	Super supper snack
10. BASIN D GANG SPEECH (4)	Fabulous fry-up!
11. D SPANISH CHIF (3)	"Salt please!"
12. U DRIPPING WHEET SPUD (3)	Chip shop special
13. BRRIANS BURR (3)	A drink! Wull's Scottish tipple!
14. REGGIE FR DOLL (3)	Great with tomato sauce

ANSWERS

MINCE AND TATTIES; BOILING BEEF; HAGGIS AND NEEPS; SCOTCH BROTH; POTTED HOUGH; PLUM PUDDING; JEELY PIECE; ICE CREAM AND JELLY; BEANS ON TOAST; EGG CHIPS AND BEANS; FISH AND CHIPS; WHITE PUDDING SUPPER; BARRS IRN BRU; FRIED EGG ROLL.

MONSTER FUN!

COME TO **BONNIE LOCH NESS** AND SEE THE MONSTER

HOW MANY THREE-LETTER WORDS CAN YOU MAKE FROM THE LETTERS IN.....

"LOCH NESS MONSTER"

The ratings are—

OVER 25 – *Excellent*
20-24 – *Good*
15-19 – *Fair*
UNDER 15 – *Try again!*

Answers: Here are 26 . . .

ROT, NOT, HOT, LOT, TOT, COT, TEN, TON, TOO, THE, LET, ONE, HER, HEN, HEM, HOE, NET, EEL, ELM, SON, SET, SEE, MEN, MET, TOE, ROE.

SPECIAL BRANCH

WULLIE'S IN A BIT OF A TANGLE! CAN YOU
HELP HIM BY WORKING OUT WHICH
BRANCH, A, B, OR C, LEADS TO THE APPLE?

BRANCH "B"
—ANSWER—

WULLIE'S DRIVING TEST

HERE'S A WEE TEST O' YER ROAD SENSE! FILL IN THIS QUESTIONNAIRE!

~ QUESTIONNAIRE ~

1. What should you have on your bike when riding at night?

Lots of carrotz tae mak ye see in the dark.

2. What do double yellow lines on the road mean?

Someone's skyted on twa bananas.

3. Where should you never cycle?

Through Mr. Gow'z allotment — he's got a big dug.

4. Why should you have a bell on your bike?

So you can ride through the park and wake Granpaw Broon up wi' it.

5. What kind of clothing should you wear when riding a bike?

A jacket wi' big pocketz — Just in case ye're passin' Mr Gow's orchard.

6. What do the following road signs mean?

 Nae smoked sausagez.

(40) Nae auld fowk.

Nae flyin' motorcycles.

IT'S THE JAIL FOR YOU, WULLIE. YE GOT THEM ALL WRANG! I HOPE THE READERS DID BETTER!

CLICK!

ANSWERS: 1. Lights (front and rear) 2. No parking 3. On the pavement. 4. To warn other road users that you are there. 5. Bright clothing 6. No U-turns; 40 mph speed limit; No motor vehicles.

JOIN THE DOTS

Join the dots from 1-63 to see exactly what's bringing Wullie out in a sweat.

ANSWER: HIS GIRLFRIEND, PRIMROSE.

AMAZE-ING

WILLIE AND HIS PALS ARE OFF TO DO A BIT OF BIRD WATCHING.
CAN YOU HELP THEM FIND THEIR WAY THROUGH THE MAZE?

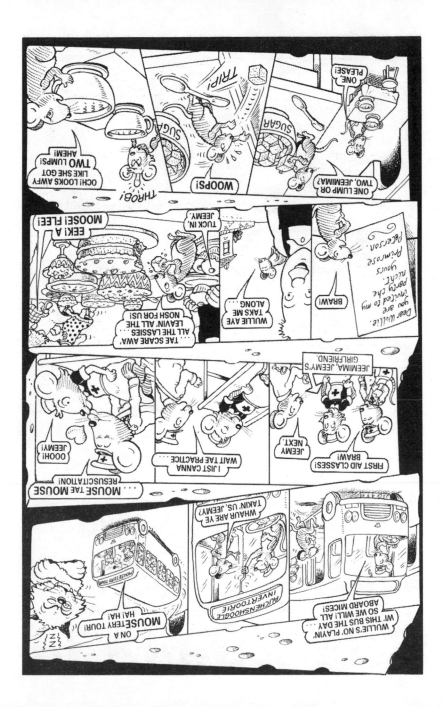

ANSWERS: MINCE, APPLE, LEMON, TREACLE, PORK

PERFECT PIES

Ma's made some pies, what's inside them is written on the top—but the letters are all mixed up. What are they?

PORK

ECTRLAE

OLENM

LEPAP

CMIEN

What Word?

CAN YOU FIND THE ONE WORD THAT CAN BE USED IN FRONT OF THESE FIVE OTHER WORDS?

STEP   HANDLE   WAY   KNOCKER   POST

ANSWER: DOOR

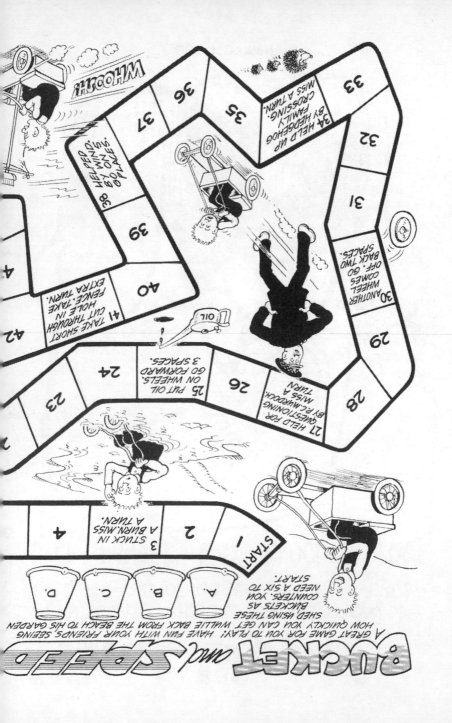

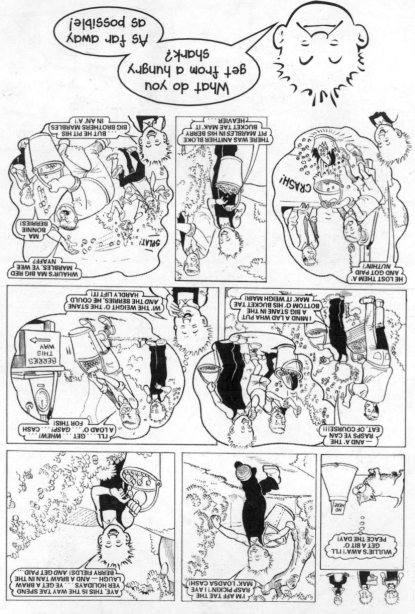

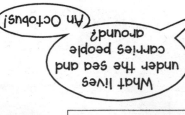

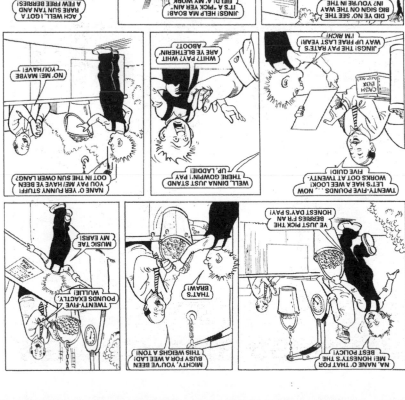

TWO OF THESE GUARDS ARE EXACTLY ALIKE.
SEE IF YOU CAN SPOT THEM.

SOLDIER ON

'KNOCK! KNOCK!
'WHO'S THERE?'
'POLICE.'
'POLICE WHO?'
'POLICE OPEN THE DOOR.'

'HAVE YOU GOT HOLES IN YOUR SOCKS?'
'OF COURSE NOT!'
'THEN HOW DO YOU GET YOUR FEET IN?'

Just Joking!

'WHAT'S GREEN AND GOES CAMPING?'
'A BRUSSELS SPROUT!'

TEACHER–'IN WHAT BATTLE WAS GENERAL WOLFE KILLED?
SUSAN; 'HIS LAST ONE, SIR.'

MUM; 'HELLO, JODIE, HAVE YOU COME BACK FOR SOMETHING YOU'VE FORGOTTEN?'
JODIE; 'NO, I'VE COME BACK FOR SOMETHING I'VE REMEMBERD!'

'WHAT IS HAIRY AND COUGHS?'
'A COCONUT WITH A COLD!'

TONI'S TEASER

SORRY, WULLIE, I'VE HIDDEN ALL YOUR FAVOURITE DISHES IN A WORDSQUARE. IF YOU CAN FIND ALL FOURTEEN I'LL GIVE YOU A FREE FISH SUPPER!

M	V	S	P	A	G	H	E	T	T	I	F
P	I	Z	Z	A	D	L	F	B	M	S	E
F	N	N	D	I	R	O	O	D	N	A	T
E	D	A	C	T	R	D	X	R	J	A	T
E	A	U	F	E	T	T	U	A	M	I	U
Y	L	L	S	H	O	R	L	R	D	H	C
R	O	T	D	C	K	N	O	I	E	S	C
F	O	I	A	R	O	K	A	P	E	U	I
R	L	L	O	R	G	N	I	R	P	S	N
I	B	A	B	E	K	R	E	N	O	D	E
T	N	O	O	D	L	E	S	F	P	L	B
S	C	I	N	K	E	N	G	A	S	A	L

MINCE ON A ROLL, FETTUCCINE, PIZZA, PAKORA, DONER KEBAB, VINDALOO, SPRING ROLL, KORMA, SUSHI, TANDOORI, STIR FRY, NOODLES, LASAGNE, SPAGHETTI.

AW, WELL, ME AN' THE READERS'LL HAE A GO ...

IT'S HAIR-RAISING!

Jings, Crivvens! Oor Wull's gone in for a richt new image! The thing is, he's no' quite sure whit tae go for so he's tried a few styles. Which two are the same?

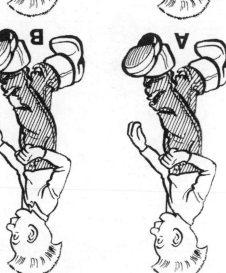

ANSWER:
C & D.

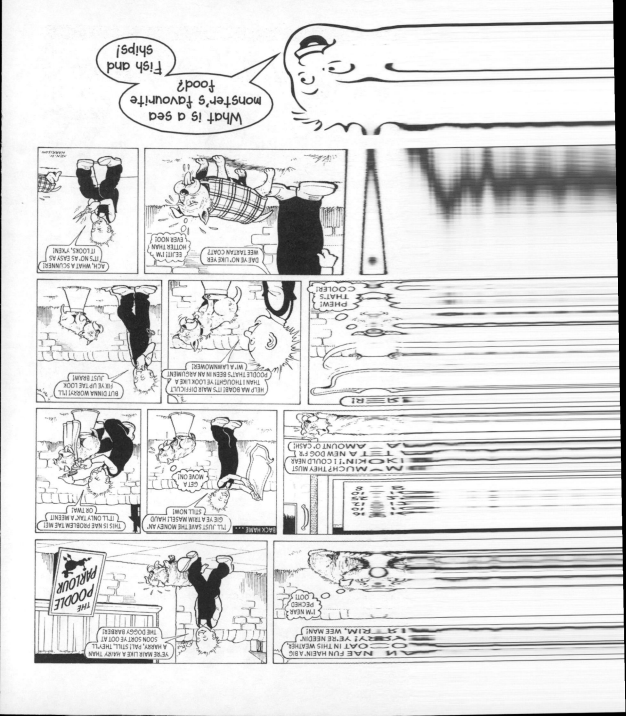

IT'S HAIR-RAISING!

Jings, Crivvens! Oor Wull's gone in for a richt new image! The thing is, he's no' quite sure whit tae go for so he's tried a few styles. Which two are the same?

A

B

C

D

E

F

ANSWER:
C & D.

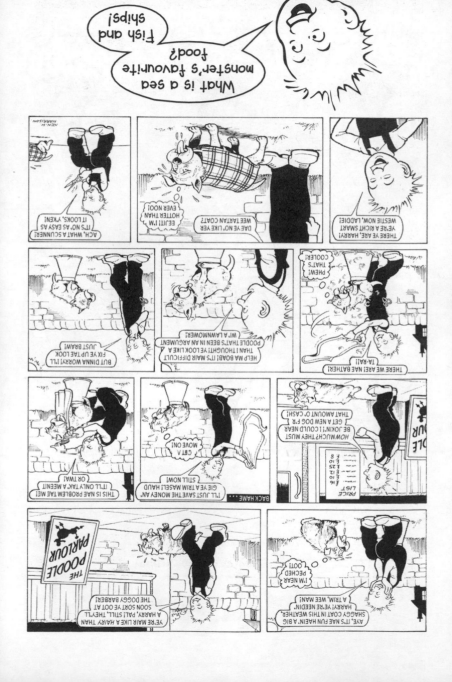

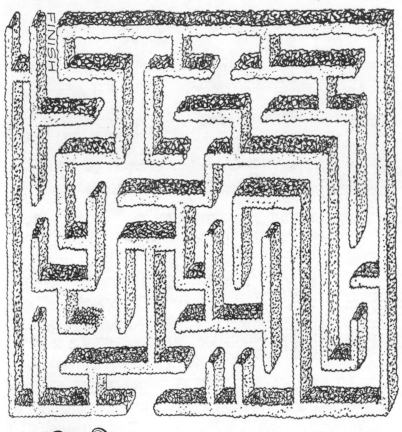

FINISH

IT'S AMAZIN'!

AYE, WULLIE'S AT IT AGAIN —
P.C. MURDOCH'S HELMET'S
NEVER SAFE WHEN HE'S
AROUND! TO ESCAPE THE
SIZE 12 TACKETTY BOOTS
OF THE LAW, WULLIE
HAS TO GET THROUGH
THE MAZE. CAN YOU
GUIDE HIM THROUGH?

MUSIC, MAESTRO, PLEASE!

CAN YOU FILL IN THE BLANKS TO REVEAL THE TITLES OF WULLIE'S TOP TWELVE SCOTTISH TUNES?

1. FLOWER of SCOTLAND
2. SCOTLAND THE BRAVE
3. MHAIRI'S ___
4. ___ BOAT SONG
5. ROWAN ___
6. MULL of KINTYRE
7. Donald WHERE'S YOUR TROOSERS
8. JOHNNY ___
9. DARK ___
10. AMAZING GRACE
11. YE CANNA SHOVE YOUR GRANNY off the BUS
12. SCHIE___

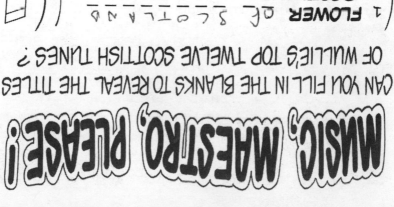

Answers:

1. Flower Of Scotland. 2. Scotland The Brave. 3. Mhairi's Wedding. 4. Skye Boat Song. 5. Rowan Tree. 6. Mull Of Kintyre. 7. Donald Where's Your Troosers. 8. Johnny Lad. 9. Dark Lochnagar. 10. Amazing Grace. 11. Ye Canna Shove Your Granny Off The Bus. 12. Schiehallion.

BACK TO FRONT

WULLIE HAS WRITTEN A MESSAGE, BUT THE ONLY PROBLEM IS, HE'S WRITTEN IT BACKWARDS! WITHOUT USING A MIRROR, CAN YOU MAKE OUT WHAT IT SAYS?

HOPE YOU ARE ALL HAVING FUN WITH THE BOOK!

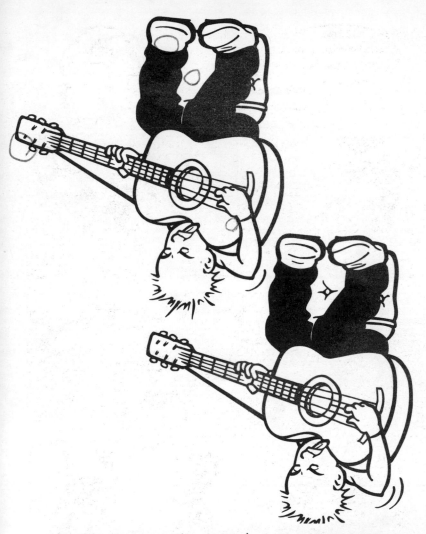

DOUBLE TROUBLE

AT FIRST GLANCE THESE TWO PICTURES OF WULLIE LOOK THE
SAME, BUT IF YOU LOOK CLOSELY YOU'LL FIND SIX
DIFFERENCES. HOW QUICKLY CAN YOU FIND THEM?

NAME GAME!

JUMBLED UP IN EACH SECTION IS A BOY'S NAME. ONCE YOU HAVE UNSCRAMBLED THEM ALL WRITE THE INITIAL LETTER OF EACH IN THE CENTRE CIRCLE. IF YOU DO IT CORRECTLY, YOU WILL HAVE ANOTHER NAME.

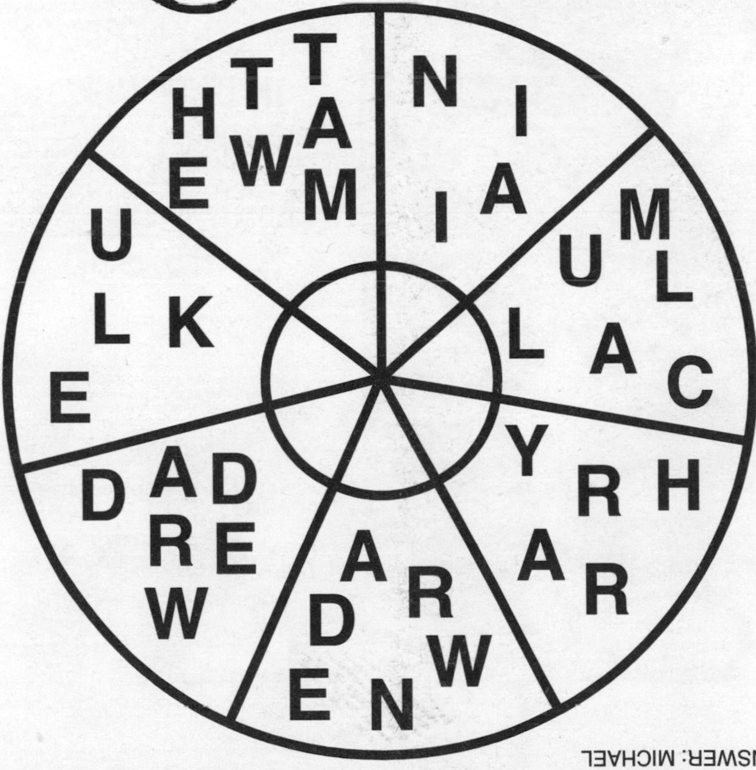

ANSWER: MICHAEL

NAMES: MATTHEW, IAIN, CALLUM, HARRY, ANDREW, EDWARD, LUKE.

HOW MANY WORDS

HOW MANY WORDS OF THREE OR MORE LETTERS CAN YOU MAKE FROM THE WORD "SCATEBOARD?"

SCORES
1-5 YOU'RE NOT TRYING!
6-11 THAT'S BETTER!
12 AND OVER—GO TO THE TOP OF THE CLASS

UNITEDS
Ayr United, Cambridge United, Carlisle United, Colchester United, Dundee United, Hartlepool United, Hereford United, Leeds United, Maidstone United, Manchester United, Newcastle United, Oxford United, Peterborough United, Rotherham United, Scunthorpe United, Sheffield United, Southend United, Torquay United, West Ham United.

CITIES
Birmingham City, Bradford City, Brechin City, Bristol City, Cardiff City, Chester City, Coventry City, Exeter City, Hull City, Leicester City, Lincoln City, Manchester City, Norwich City, Stoke City, Swansea City, York City.   **—:Answers**

CAN YOU NAME AT LEAST 10 "UNITEDS" AND 10 "CITIES" IN THE ENGLISH AND SCOTTISH LEAGUES?

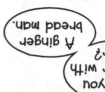

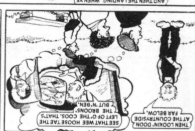

There's a Moose Loose

STARRING 'JEEMY'

Aboot the Hoose!

JINGS! WHIT A WIND!

WHEW! AHM GLAD TAE BE OOT O' THE STORMY BLAST.

I DINNA LIKE STOOR LYIN' ABOOT.

WHEEE!

JEST A MINUTE

Whit kind o' cars come frae Norway?
Fiords!

Why would Wullie no' study history?
He thocht it better tae let bygones be bygones!

Whit's the difference between a cuddy and a postage stamp?
Ane ye lick wi' a stick, an' the ither ye stick wi' a lick!

Whit is rhubarb?
Celery wi' a red face!

If ye cross an' owl an' a goat whit dae ye get?
A hootenanny!

Whit's worse than rainin' cats an' dogs?
Hailin' taxis!

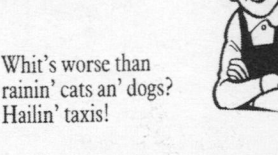

Answer: Path c

TANGLED TRAILS
WHICH PATH LEADS WULLIE TO HIS BUCKET?

A B C

Jumbled Words

THESE MUSICAL INSTRUMENTS ARE ALL JUMBLED UP!
SEE HOW QUICKLY YOU CAN UNSCRAMBLE THEM ALL!

POAIN   EFUTL   ESIPBGAP   HONAMUHTGR   SMRUD

ANSWERS: PIANO FLUTE BAGPIPES MOUTHORGAN DRUMS

WHICH PIECE OF TILING WILL FIT INTO THE FLOOR!

A.

B

C.

D.

Answer:—
B

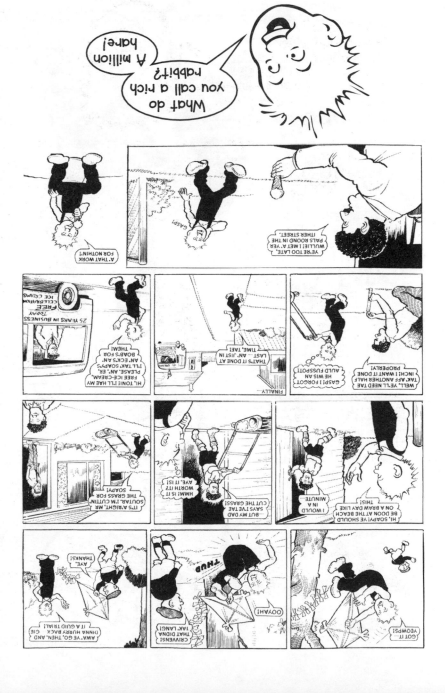

JUMBLED JUICES

WULLIE'S FEELING THE HEAT! TO COOL HIMSELF DOWN, HE'S THINKING OF NICE COLD DRINKS OF JUICES. CAN YOU UNSCRAMBLE THE LETTERS TO FIND THEM ALL?

GOAENR   PAPEL

MOLNE   OGMAN

YBRCABNRE

PRGAIETUFR

ANSWERS
ORANGE APPLE LEMON
GRAPEFRUIT MANGO
CRANBERRY

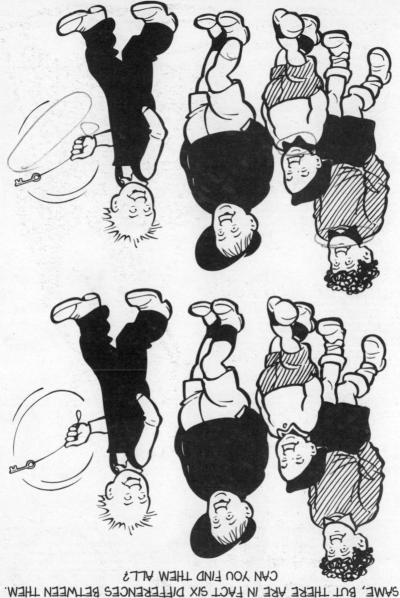

SPOT THE DIFFERENCE

THESE TWO PICTURES OF WULLIE AND HIS PALS MIGHT LOOK THE
SAME, BUT THERE ARE IN FACT SIX DIFFERENCES BETWEEN THEM.
CAN YOU FIND THEM ALL?

WULLIE'S WORLD

THE CANADIAN GOOSE HAS A WINGSPAN OF SIX FEET AND CAN FLY NON-STOP HUNDREDS OF MILES AT A RATE OF 55 MILES PER HOUR. WHY DO GEESE FLY IN A V SHAPED WEDGE? IN ORDER TO CUT DOWN ON WIND RESISTANCE!

PUDDOCK: EATS FLECHS, BIDES IN JEELY JAR. BRAW FOR FLEGGIN' PRIMROSE PATTERSON.

THE ANGELFISH IS A POPULAR FRESH-WATER FAVOURITE OF PEOPLE WITH HOME AQUARIUMS. MOST ANGELFISH ARE SMALL (8 INCHES LONG), BUT SOME DO GROW TO TWO FEET IN LENGTH. THE FISH RESEMBLES THE SHAPE OF A FLINT ARROWHEAD.

THE SEVERAL VARIETIES OF GIRAFFES ARE DISTINGUISHED BY THE DIFFERENCES IN THE COLOUR AND PATTERNS OF THEIR COATS.

OF TREES, BY USING THEIR LONG (17 INCH) TONGUES.

GIRAFFES ARE THE TALLEST ANIMALS. SOME MALE GIRA-FFES GROW TO A HEIGHT OF OVER 18 FEET. THEY FEED MAINLY ON LEAVES AND BRANCHES

P.C. MURDOCH'S BUDGIE: COLOUR, BLUE WITH COPPER RING. FAVOURITE SAYINGS, "EVENING ALL," AND "NOW THEN WHIT'S A' THIS?"

OF NATURE

SCOTTISH MOOSE: SMALLEST MEMBER OF THE MOOSE FAMILY. BIDES IN HOLE, EATS CHEESE. ANSWERS TO JEEMY, SOMETIMES.

THE MOOSE IS THE LARGEST MEMBER OF THE DEER FAMILY, MEASURING OVER 9 FEET IN HEIGHT. HOWEVER THE MOOSE'S NECK IS SO SHORT THAT IT MUST KNEEL TO FEED ON LOW PLANTS. EACH YEAR THE MOOSE GROWS A NEW SET OF ANTLERS.

THE GREAT HORNED OWL IS THE LARGEST AND FIERCEST OF THE OWL FAMILY. THIS CREATURE CAN LIVE IN ALL TYPES OF ENVIRONMENTS, FROM DENSE FORESTS TO BARREN DESERTS.
THE GREAT HORNED OWL HAS A VORACIOUS APPETITE, FEEDING ON RABBITS, SKUNKS, MICE, AS WELL AS BIRDS.
BECAUSE OF THE CONSTRUCTION OF ITS WINGS, THE OWL IS ABLE TO FLY IN ABSOLUTE SILENCE.

HARRY: ORIGINALLY FROM THE WEST HIGHLANDS, LIKES BONES. DISNAE LIKE CATS. SOMETIMES KNOWN AS WULL'S BEST FRIEND.

CAN YOU SPOT TWO IDENTICAL SANDCASTLES?

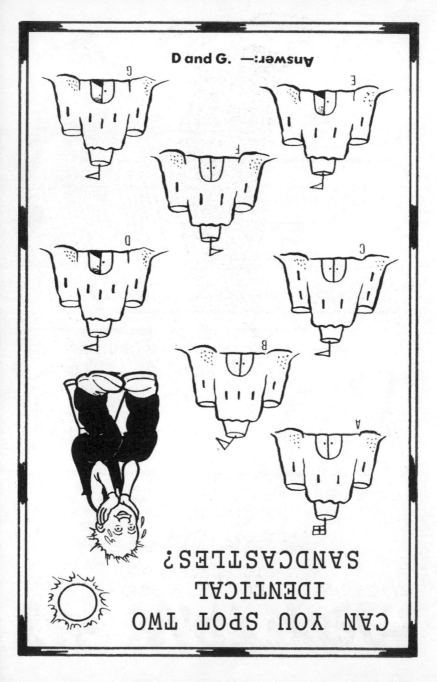

Answer:— D and G.

HOW MANY WORDS

HOW MANY WORDS OF THREE LETTERS OR MORE CAN
YOU FIND FROM THE WORD

NEWSPAPER?

SCORE

15–20 – WHO'S A BRAINBOX   8–14 – STILL GOOD
1–7 – BETTER LUCK NEXT TIME!

WORD PUZZLE

IF YOU ANSWER THE FOLLOWING CLUES CORRECTLY, THE LETTERS IN THE SHADED BOXES WILL SPELL THE NAME OF ONE OF WULLIE'S FAVOURITE SPORTS. WE HAVE GIVEN YOU A FEW LETTERS TO HELP YOU.

1. ONE OF WULLIE'S PALS
2. YOU DRY YOURSELF WITH THESE
3. FROZEN WATER
4. WARM SEASON
5. CARTOON HERO
6. FISH AND?
7. HARD-WORKING INSECT
8. COLOUR

S	O	A	**P**	Y
T	O	W	E	L	**S**
		I	C	**E**
S	U	M	M	**E**	R
B	A	T	M	A	N
C	H	I	**P**	S
A	N	**T**
G	R	E	E	**N**

ANSWERS
1.SOAPY 2.TOWELS 3.ICE
4.SUMMER 5.BATMAN 6.CHIPS
7.ANT 8.GREEN
THE SPORT IS SWIMMING

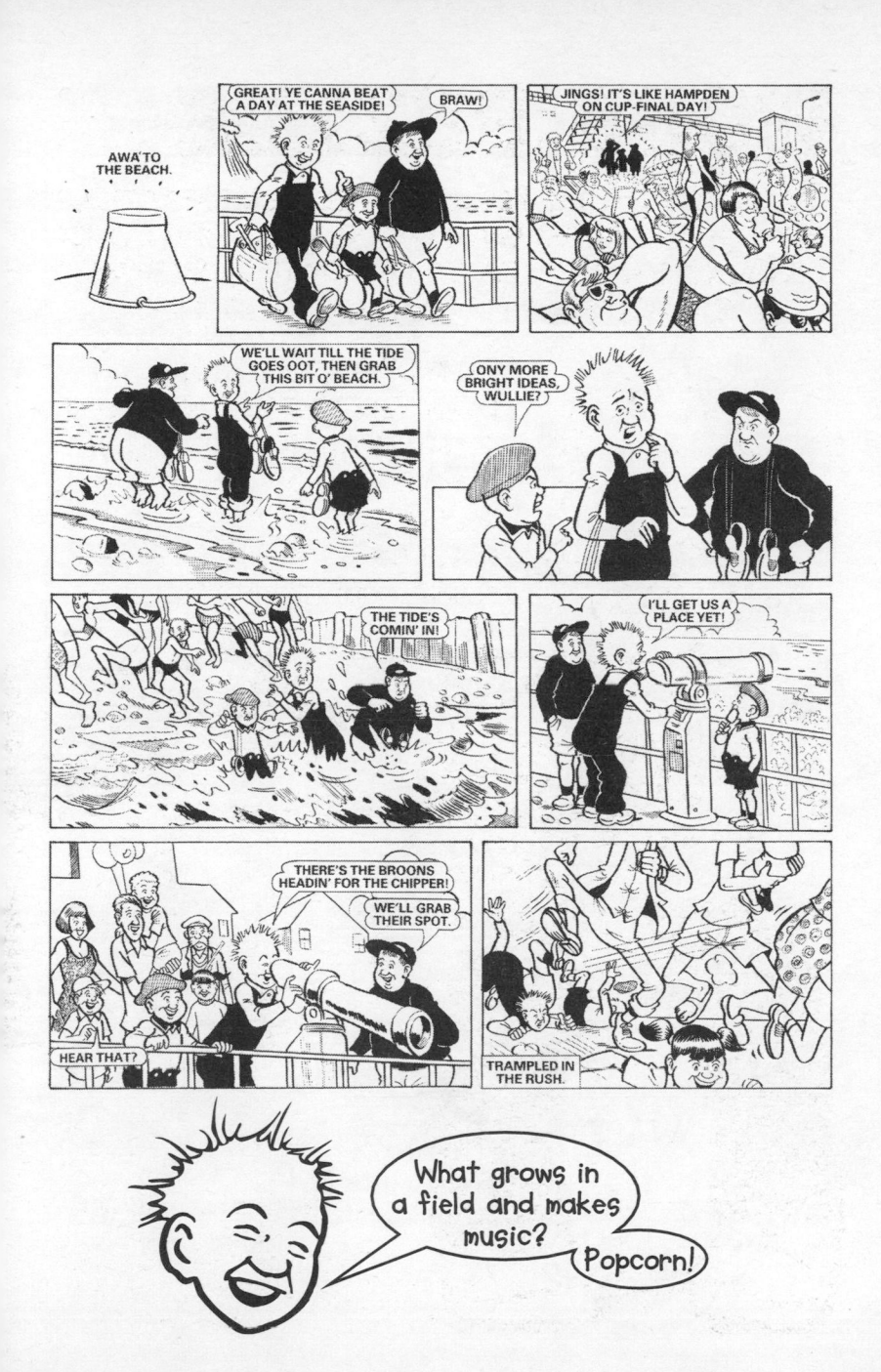

Just Joking!

NAME NINE ANIMALS FROM AFRICA?
'EIGHT ELEPHANTS AND A GIRAFFE!'

WHY DID THE INVISIBLE MAN LOOK IN THE MIRROR?
TO SEE IF HE STILL WASN'T THERE!

WHAT LIVES UNDER THE WATER AND WEARS A COWBOY HAT?
BILLY THE SQUID!

WHAT DO YOU GET WHEN YOU JUMP IN THE RED SEA?
WET!

'DOCTOR, DOCTOR, I KEEP THINKING I'M A GOAT!'
'HOW LONG HAVE YOU FELT LIKE THIS?'
'SINCE I WAS A KID!'

'WAITER, WAITER, THIS SOUP TASTES FUNNY!'
'SO WHY AREN'T YOU LAUGHING?'

QUIZ BIZ!

Thinking caps on for this one!

1. What are the names of Wullie's three best pals? *Soapy*

2. Culloden Moor, scene of the 1746 battle is near which city? *INVERNESS*

3. Near which town are THE SUMMER ISLES? *Ullapool*

4. Where in Scotland would you find the Scott Monument? *Edinburgh.*

5. Which is Scotland's longest railway bridge? *TAY*

6. Which football team plays at Pitoddrie? *ABERDEEN*

7. On which date do we celebrate Hogmanay? *31 DECEMBER*

8. What is the name of the Queen's official residence in Scotland?

9. Which ocean separates Britain from America? *ATLANTIC*

10. Which Scot wrote the song "Auld Lang Syne"? *Robert Burns*

Answers 1. Fat Bob, Soapy, Eck. 2. Inverness. 3. Ullapool. 4. Princes Street, Edinburgh. 5. The Tay Railway Bridge. 6. Aberdeen. 7. 31st December. 8. Holyrood Palace. 9. Atlantic. 10. Robert Burns.

SQUARE UP!

With the help of the grid, complete the other half of this drawing of Oor Wullie.

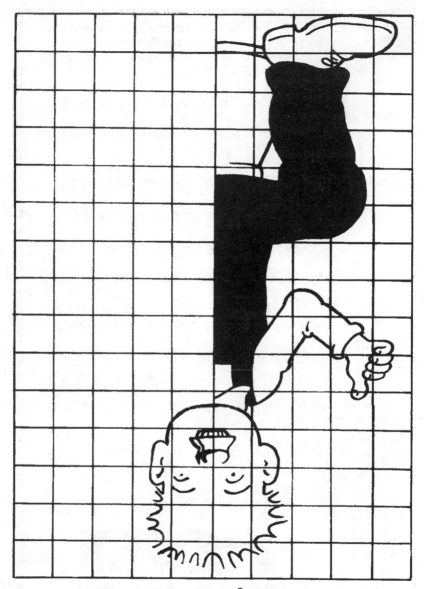

SMILE!

WULLIE! THESE PHOTOGRAPHS ARE DELIGHTFUL!

P-PRIMROSE!

GIES A LOOK!

IT LOOKS LIKE WULLIE'S TAKEN THE PLUNGE AND HAD HIS PASSPORT PHOTO TAKEN! CAN YOU TELL WHICH TWO OF THE SIX PICTURES ARE THE SAME?

2 AND 6 ARE THE SAME